SOLDIERING ON

Also by Vernon Scannell

A Mortal Pitch (1957)

Masks of Love (1960)

(Heinemann Award for Literature, 1960)

A Sense of Danger (1962)

(Recommended by the Poetry Book Society)

Walking Wounded (1965)

Epithets of War (1969)

Selected Poems (1971)

The Winter Man (1973)

The Loving Game (1975)

(Poetry Book Society Choice)

A Proper Gentleman (1977)

New & Collected Poems 1950–1980 (1980)

Winterlude (1982)

Funeral Games (1987)

Soldiering On

Poems of Military Life

Vernon Scannell

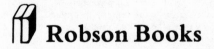 Robson Books

First published in Great Britain in 1989 by Robson Books Ltd,
Bolsover House, 5–6 Clipstone Street, London W1P 7EB
Copyright © 1989 Vernon Scannell

British Library Cataloguing in Publication Data
Scannell, Vernon, *1922–*
    Soldiering on: poems of military life.
    I. Title
    821'. 914
ISBN 0 86051 376 9

Printed in Great Britain by
St Edmundsbury Press Ltd, Bury St Edmunds, Suffolk

Contents

Acknowledgements are due to the editors of *Ambit*, the *London Magazine*, and the *Spectator* where some of these poems first appeared; also to BBC Radio 3's Poetry Now.

Reveille

The vitreous dawn is smashed by noise.
The rooster bugler calls out cock-a-hoop;
Dreams break, the pieces drift away,
Quick glimpses of unmilitary things –
White softnesses and silks and secret hair –
Before the coarse and iron-booted Now
Stamps hard and crushes
All such daintinesses in the dirt
And shouts the brute day in.
Blind fingers fumble for fag-ends and then
The overture of coughs and groans begins.
Sergeant someone slams into the hut,
Hoarse muezzin who cries again
The formal exhortations of his faith:
Wakey-wakey! . . .Rise and shine!
Drop your cocks and grab your socks
It's re-vall-ee!

Getting Fell In

Get fell in you dozey men!
The Corporal roars.
The khaki bundles clomp from huts
On dubbined boots and get fell in
Beneath a sky of stone
Unfriendly as the barrack square
They clatter on.
The bundles coalesce, are one.
Scorched porridge sniffs the air.
Squad... .stand-at . . .Ease!
Squad . . .shun!
Move to the right in threes! Right . . .turn!
By the left . . .quick . . .march!
Lay-rye . . .lay-rye . . .lay!
The section moves, brown caterpillar,
Feculent plump worm,
With chink and clink of eating irons,
To break the fast of night,
First fodder of the day.

Fixing Bayonets

On the command 'Fix!' you don't fix.
Do you understand, you dozey men?
That man that looks as if he's shitting bricks,
Stand up straight and properly to attention,
Left thumb in line with seam, chest out, chin in!
You might have broke your mother's heart my lad
But mine you'll never break! Now, listen Squad:
On the command 'Fix', as I just said,
You don't fix. Listen. What you do instead
Is with your left hand seize your bayonet-handle,
Knuckles to the front without no fumble
As with your right you shove the muzzle out
In front of you like this, and then you wait
For my command of 'Bayonets!' When I shout
This order out you whip your bayonet from
The scabbard and fix it into place. And there
You stay, your left hand at the spout, the palm
Turned in towards you. Wait until you hear
The next word of command and this will be
To bring you to attention. That quite clear?
You understand the drill? Well, we'll soon see.
Squad . . .stand-at . . .ease! Squad . . .shun! Now squad
    will fix
Bayonets . . .Squad . . .Fix! . . .Oh my God,
As you were! You shower of useless pricks!
Can't you understand? On my command
Of 'Fix' you silly sods you do *not* fix.
Squad . . .as you were! Squad . . .shun! We'll get it right
Even if I keep you here all night.

Bayonet Training

From far away, a mile or so,
The wooden scaffolds could be seen
    On which fat felons swung;
But closer view showed these to be
Sacks, corpulent with straw and tied
    To beams from which they hung.

The sergeant halted his platoon.
'Right lads,' he barked, 'you see them sacks?
    I want you to forget
That sacks is what they are and act
As if they was all Jerries – wait!
    Don't move a muscle yet!

'I'm going to show you how to use
The bayonet as it should be done.
    If any of you feel
Squeamish like, I'll tell you this:
There's one thing Jerry just can't face
    And that thing is cold steel.

'So if we're going to win this war
You've got to understand you must
    Be brutal, ruthless, tough.
I want to hear you scream for blood
As you rip out his guts and see
    The stuff he had for duff.

'Remember this. You're looking at
A bunch of Jerries over there.
  They'd kill you if they could,
And fuck your sisters, mother too.
You've got to stop the bastards, see?
  I hope that's understood.

'All right? Platoon, in your own time,
Fix your bayonets; stand at ease
  Then watch my moves with care.
First, the High Port, done like this:
You cant the rifle straight across
  Your chest and hold it there.

'Note the angle: left hand firm
Around the barrel, half-way down.
  The right hand grasps the small.
Whatever happens never change
Your grip upon your weapon. No!
  I don't mean that at all!

'You dirty-minded little sods!
The next position – that's On Guard –
  You swing the bayonet out
In front of you like this, chest high,
Take one pace forward with your left
  Knee bent. Let's see you try.

'High Port! On Guard! High Port! On Guard!
All right. You've got the rough idea.
  Stand easy and keep still.
And now – Delivery of the Point –
In other words the moment when
  You go in for the kill.

'So watch me now and listen good.
I'll want to hear you yell like me,
    So take a good deep breath
Before you stick the bayonet in.
If you don't kill him with the blade
    You'll scare the sod to death!'

The young recruits stood there and watched
And listened as their tutor roared
    And stabbed his lifeless foe;
Their faces were expressionless,
Impassive as the winter skies
    Black with threats of snow.

Perimeter Guard

His second two-hour duty: the wind
Is now stropped to such
Fine and steely sharpness that
It might slice off a shrivelled lobe or finger.
The stars are brilliant chippings of frozen flint,
Beautiful, but quite indifferent
To sublunar hurt.

His stunned toes are welded together;
He is club-footed
By the weather. The only
Nostrum for such misery and loneliness
Is found in fantasies of somewhere other,
A feminine place, not erotic
But warm, motherly.

Lavender-scented pillow and sheets;
No gruff blankets there:
Soft wool, a cool counterpane
Of candlewick that soothed an infant fever;
Sweet, unsnoring dark. He shuts his eyes against
The stars' impersonal derision
And the wind's malice.

Then dream and the silence are broken
By a sound beyond
The wire and his eyes are filled
With star-sparks like frozen tears; unsure he calls

'Halt! Who goes there?' No one answers. The glitter
Melts from his eyes; then he hears the wind
Whisper: 'Foe!...Foe!...Foe!...'

Lights Out

The pyramids of canvas shrink,
And palely gleam,
Draw closer to each other
As the night
Slips wedges of the dark between.
A steam of mist
Sways above the grasses
Where, like slanted beams of light,
Guy-ropes hide their ends.
Silence is a black sky; then
A sudden burst of sound
Is hung there goldenly, slides down
And then soars back and spreads.

Here is a sadness to confound,
The throat of brass
Is hoarse with centuries of ache;
And, waking or asleep,
We all recall
Bereavements, near or distant, feel
The tears in things.

Then, later, as the tall
Sergeant of the daylight calls
All sections on parade,
The griefs of night are laid aside,
Though they are not mislaid.

TROOPSHIP

1 *Setting Sail*

Leaving Greenock, on a slaty day
When sea and sky profess the same patched grey
Of jankers denim or of prison walls
And fussy tugboats answer seagulls' calls,
All other-ranks are ranged along the rails
To wave goodbye to Blighty's hills and vales –
'Hill and vales my arse!' as they would say:
Back streets of Glasgow, Leeds and Tiger Bay
Are what they'll dream about when they're at sea,
The loci of their shared mythology
Of sexy, willing women and complete
Freedom and success in civvy street.

The coastline melts in mist. The ship rides on
To where the waiting convoy lolls upon
The queasy seas. Destroyers prowl and wink
Quick signals; lean corvettes appear, then sink
And rise again like whippets in high corn;
The horns of merchantmen and tankers warn
The world of darknesses all sailors know.
The swaddies turn away and go below.

The voyage has begun: that is to say
The physical adventure through the spray
And lurching waves beneath which killers lurk –
The guttural U-Boats glide through wavering mirk
Where mines like huge black conker-cases float –
But other voyages begin, each boat
Small tub of flesh and spirit, each a *Me*
That drifts in waters other than this sea,

16

Trawling the past, or future fantasy,
For brief reprieve from this reality;
The remora, that piscine limpet-mine,
But one unprimed, its amiable design
To keep the vessel safe in anodyne
And friendly seas, may save a few, but more
Will run aground on that unfriendly shore
Where present terrors from the rocks are aimed,
And must be faced and recognised and named.

2 *Letters Home*

1

Dear Mum and Dad,
                      We're on the high seas now.
I don't know when you'll get to see this note.
I just asked Sergeant MacNamara how
They got the mail to Blighty from a boat
Like this. He says we stop at Gib – we hope –
And mail is put ashore and then flown back.
I'd like to climb inside this envelope
And whizz straight home inside a postman's sack.
I'm kidding really. Life at sea's all right.
The grub's not bad. You're not to worry, Mum.
We're safe as houses here, so you sleep tight
And bet your boots that we will overcome
Our enemies on land and sea. And Dad,
It won't be very long before we drink
A few more pints than what we've ever had
Before. I hope this finds you in the pink –
That's what they used to say in your old war,
Right, Dad? You came safe back and I will too,
So don't you fret. Remember this is your
Lucky lad, the boy you always knew
Would land the right way up. Good night, God bless,
Remember me to Auntie Flo and Dave.
And thank you both for all the happiness
And love and caring that you always gave –
Sounds soft, I know – But still I'm glad it's said.
Night-night again. Keep smiling.
                                  Love from Fred.

2

Darling Jane,
        I thought I wouldn't write
Until we're off this floating lavatory
But find I just can't face another night
Unless I scribble something you will see
And knowing this brings you an inch or two
Closer, that is all.
        The other chaps
Are either being sick or telling 'true'
Tales of conquests, then producing snaps
Of wives or girlfriends contradicting their
Boasts of smashing bints and lovely tarts –
Just ordinary girls with mousy hair
And little, cautious eyes that all the arts
Of camera and make-up can't disguise.
I felt an urge to join them and to show
Your picture, but I knew this was unwise
And kept away of course. 'You'll never know
How much I love you' - that's their favourite song,
Or one of them. They sing it through the nose
With much vibrato. Yes, I know it's wrong
To patronise, but how do you suppose
I manage to keep sane? The only way
That works is packing all perceptions in
The salt of irony. And please don't say
It's all my fault, by now I could have been
An officer and gent. I know it's true,
But do believe me when I say I'm not
Perversely setting out to worry you
Or test your love, nor am I showing what
They call 'inverted snobbery'. It's just

That I can't take the farce of rank that's based
On privilege and class. I no more trust
My leaders than I would myself if faced
By those appalling choices war presents.
But don't you worry, darling. I shall pray
That none of God's sadistic jokes prevents
Our being re-united one fine day –
Though who or what I'll pray to isn't clear.
My love, I miss you and I hope that you
Miss me a little too. The words I hear,
Though scented and banal, are not untrue.
Do you remember Burns's lovely song,
'A Red Red Rose'? 'Till a' the seas gang dry . . .'
Well let us hope it won't be quite that long
Before we are together
                              Always,
                                    Guy.

3

Dearest Darling Peg,
                          You just can't guess
How much I miss you. All I do is think
About the way you looked in that blue dress
You wore at Mum's. I never sleep a wink
Without I dream that I am cuddling you
And sometimes doing other things. I bet
That you can guess what they might be! I do
Love you sweetheart. Ever since we met
That night at the Astoria when I

Asked you for a dance and you agreed
I fell in love and couldn't make out why
You seemed to feel the same. I'll always need
Your love my sweet and hope that you'll need mine.
Remember my last leave? The time they played
That smashing song of Vera Lynn's? The shine
Your eyes had was so beautiful it made
My heart melt like a snowball in the sun.
Don't look at any man while I'm away.
It won't be long before the war is won
And I'll be back. Every night I pray
It won't be long and that you'll wait for me.
I wish now we'd got married when we could.
There's nothing in the world I'd rather be
Than your life's love and care for you for good.
The only thing that stopped me was the thought
That with me on a draft going overseas
And facing action and all that we ought
To wait in case – your Mum and Dad agrees –
In case – you know – I didn't come safe through.
You're not to worry love. Of course I will.
How could I not when I've the thought of you
Waiting there? So I'll be yours until
The end of time. Remember Vera's song,
Yours till the birds fail to sing? I'll be back
My darling love. Let's pray it won't be long.
A million loving kisses
                    from
                         Your Jack.

4

Dear Old Bunty,
                          Just a hurried line
To tell you all goes well. The men are fine.
No problems over discipline. I feel
That all, or most, of them are made of steel,
And British steel at that. *Esprit de corps*
Could not be better. Roger is a bore
But knows his job and keeps out of my way.
The younger officers are keen and they,
I'm sure, won't let me down.
                          Keep well my dear,
We'll give the Hun a thrashing, never fear.
Hope you've got some grazing for the mare;
That fellow Jenkins must have land to spare.
My love to both the girls and cousin Maud,
And most of all to you,
                          Your husband,
                                    Claude.

5

Dear Gladys,
                          Hope you're well. The kiddies too.
I never was a one for writing letters
As well you know. This ship is like a zoo
And I'm head-keeper. Some should be in fetters,
I mean those lads that think they're on a cruise
And all they're here to do is lark about,
And think they haven't got a thing to lose
Because we're out at sea. But they'll find out.
I'll get them on the boat-deck for a spell

Of pack-drill at the double. Then they'll see
I'm still the boss and I know how to quell
Their bolshie little tricks. They think CB
Can't be awarded on a ship. They're right.
We're all confined to barracks in a way.
But I can think up punishments a sight
Worse than what CB is any day.
I'm their Sergeant-Major and they must
Recognise that what I say is law.
That's the way you build the kind of trust
You've got to have in action. Major Shaw
Is like most officers, not hard enough.
But he's not bad. The subalterns are all
Wet behind the ears. When things get rough
I'll have to hold their hands. They're what I call
More gentleman than officer. I mean
They've got posh voices and all that but no
Leadership. One's only just nineteen
And thinks he's still at school. He'll have to grow
To manhood quick when we go up the blue.
The other day he called me 'Sir' then tried
To act as if he hadn't, but he knew
I'd heard him and he blushed up like a bride.
Well, Glad, I reckon this is just about
The longest letter that I ever wrote.
If Billy's naughty give him one good clout
And tell him that his Dad will make a note
Of all his bad behaviour and he'll pay
When I get back. A hug and kiss for Lil
And lots saved up for you until the day
That I come home.
                           Your loving husband,
                               Bill.

6

Dear Mother,
                    Just a little note to say
That all is well and that you need not fuss.
The food is good, my quarters are OK,
Though Sergeant-Major Sharp's an awkward cuss
And sometimes makes me feel a frightful ass.
He's one of the survivors of Dunkirk
And served in India on the Khyber Pass
Or some such place. I just don't like his smirk
Whenever I inspect my chaps or when
I give a little pep-talk on morale.
He doesn't even hide it from the men.
It's so embarrassing. I think I shall
Quite firmly tick him off. Well anyway
I mustn't bore you talking army shop.
Everything's been peaceful till today.
Just half an hour ago we had to drop
Some depth-charges which means a hostile sub
Is prowling pretty close. I don't suppose
The Navy boys will let him sink our tub.
Let's hope they're wide awake and on their toes.
Regards to all chums at the tennis club,
My love to Jill and send me one of those
Curly briar pipes, you know the kind
That Sherlock Holmes was always seen to smoke
Though his, I think, was meerschaum. Never mind
If they are scarce or you are feeling broke;
I've no doubt I'll survive without.
                                        Well, mums,
I'd better finish this. I've lots to do.
Don't think I sit here twiddling idle thumbs –
First, boat-drill, then a lecture to sit through.
They keep us on the trot. Now don't you let

The rationing and air-raids get you down.
I know the war is far from over yet
But we'll come through, and won't we paint the town
Fifty shades of red when I come back!
First, the job in hand! then fun and games.
Keep smiling mother. Remember me to Mac
And Mrs P.
                With lots of love from
                                James.

7

Dear Ron,
                Well, here I am at sea. I bet
You never thought the sods would ever get
Yours truly on a troopship. Nor did I.
The buggers had an escort standing by
To pick me up as soon as I got out –
Full magazines, one ready up the spout:
They'd a shot me through the bollocks if I'd run!
Handcuffs too. What else could I a done
But go along with them? I tried to slip
The cuffs. No dice. They got me on the ship
Before they took them off and even then
I never moved a step without two men
Detailed as my escort till we got
Out of sight of land. I don't know what
They thought I'd do – dive overboard, I guess,
And swim three miles or so in battledress.
Not likely mate! But don't think I'll agree
To join the true-blue warriors and be
A willing dish of cannon-fodder. Me,
I'm going to stay alive and let the rest

Get blown to Kingdom Come. It's maybe best
For me to say no more – you never know
Who gets to read your mail. I've got to go
And see old Holy Joe for what he calls
'A little friendly chat'. A load of balls
Is what I call it. Still, I'll get a smoke
And cup of chah. He's not a bad old bloke,
An old brown-hatter if he had the guts.
You know the type: straight out of *Comic Cuts*,
All Adam's apple, teeth and great big ears
And with that silly smile you get with queers.
It's funny how they fancy us hard men
And wouldn't swap one wicked sod for ten
Well-behaved lance-corporals.
                                          Well, I hope
You'll soon be out the nick. I know you'll cope
With all the bullshit that they dish out there.
We'll meet up, you and me, some time, somewhere,
And have the greatest piss-up ever was.
Don't let the bastards grind you down because
You're worth more than a million of them, Ronnie.
Okay?
            Keep smiling.
                                 Your old china,
                                          Johnny.

8

Dear Hilda,
                  Goodness knows when you'll see this
Or where I'll be when you are reading it.
You simply can't imagine how I miss

26

Our times together when we used to sit
After evensong with Ovaltine
And chocolate biscuits in those halcyon days
Before this beastly war. I do not mean
I'm sorry I joined up though there are ways,
I now believe, in which I could have served
Both God and country more effectively
At home. The trouble is I'm too reserved,
Too *different* from the men who come to me
For help or comfort. They can't understand
My language or my values, nor I theirs –
They might be natives of a different land.
One of them's just left. He sits and stares
And smokes my cigarettes and might as well
Be a chimpanzee for all the sense
Of contact that I feel. I tried to tell
Him something of God's mercy and immense
Capacity for loving even those
Most sinful and debased. I should explain:
This soldier, Johnny Evans – broken nose
And shifty eyes – was handcuffed on the train
In case he ran away. He's what he calls
A real Detention Wallah, spent more time,
He proudly claims, behind the Glasshouse walls
Than with his regiment. His only crime,
As far as I can see, consists in his
Failure to conform and toe the line.
I tried to tell him how the sinner is
Most dear to God. I quoted Karl Barth's fine
Sermon on what he has called the First
Christian Fellowship – the thieves nailed there
With Christ, enduring agony and thirst
As great as His, sharing His despair,
Not knowing they would finally attain
Life everlasting. Jesus did not choose

27

To die with those who knew what they would gain;
His partners were the scum of slums and stews,
The most despised – oh Hilda, please excuse
My preaching on like this! Truth is, I feel
That men like Evans show that I'm no use
At all as Padre. When I said, 'Let's Kneel
And say a simple prayer together, pray
For help and guidance in the strife to come',
He said, 'No thanks. I'd best be on my way.
But don't mind me. And say one for my mum.
She swallows all that stuff.' I could have wept.
The strange thing is he makes me feel so weak,
So lacking in experience, inept
And somehow less than masculine; a freak.
Ah well, forgive these feeble bleatings, dear.
Things might improve when we are under fire.
I've been assured there's nothing quite like fear
Of sudden death or maiming to inspire
Religious feelings. Only yesterday
Sergeant-Major Sharp was heard to say
There's nothing like old Jerry's eighty-eights
To make a whole battalion start to pray.
Evans says that he'll put on his skates
Long before he gets in range of guns.
I think that he perhaps exaggerates
His lack of spirit. He said that he who runs
Away lives to run another day.
Such cynicism – but I ramble on.
Please give my kind regards to George and tell
Him that I'm sure that he, if anyone,
Will care for my parishioners as well
Or better than I did.
                              Must choose a hymn
For church parade.
                              Goodnight, God bless,
                                        from Tim.

3 *Port of Arrival*

It is like coming back to somewhere known,
Or dreamed about for years, its features grown
Familiar yet imprecise, now blurred
By frequent fingering, observed and heard
But in another life. The place we see
Is just as we imagined it would be
Except its furnishings are somehow less
Spectacular, more drab, and we confess
To disappointment, something like a sense
Of loss, of being cheated. The difference
Between the cherished image and the real
Is that of tone. Unlike our bright ideal
The buildings we see now are not pure white
But ochre with a hint of pink; the light
Is not that pale and deliquescent gold,
But harsh, acescent, and it does not hold
Expected spicy perfumes but the scent
Of urine, sweat, and various excrement.
And yet the sky's fresh, smoothly-ironed blue
Is as we knew it would be, and the few
Dusty palm trees near the jabbering quay
Are those dark frozen fountains they should be.
The women, in their long black robes, conceal
Behind their yashmaks all they think and feel
And, like the fellahin, appear to be
Models for the scriptural pictures we
Remember on the walls of Sunday School.
Incongruous beside them, stands the cool
And polished Captain with his little squad
Of other-ranks, less elegantly shod
And clad, who stand at ease in front of rows

Of stationary trucks. Two camels doze
Like dusty hillocks mounted on thin props.
Hoarse shouts and rattlings, then the gangway drops.
The order comes for us to disembark
And, like the crowd emerging from a dark
Cinema, we blink as we see sores
And milky, sightless eyes, wounds, not from wars,
But death and ignorance. The beggars' cry
Despairingly demands baksheesh. The sky
Remains serene, its smooth indifference spreads
A seamless canopy above our heads,
Nor does that bland composure seem to feel
The presence of the great dark birds that wheel
And drift on lazy, outstretched wings which throw
Their black prophetic shadows here below;
And, while no smear of threatening cloud appears,
Faint thunder whispers in our wondering ears.

Swearing In

What a fucking awful mob,
The Gordon fucking Highlanders.
That fucking bastard sergeant, I'll
Smack him in the fucking gob –
   He's put me on a fucking fizzer
For sweet fuck-all the rotten fucker.
I'll kill the fucker, so I will.
I'm on a fucking charge tomorrow –
   it's fucking pay parade an' all –
   and I'll be on a C fucking B,
Seven fucking days at least – what for?
Just for being fucking me.
An idle boot-lace, that's what he
Pegged me for the rotten fucker,
Idle boot-lace? Was it fuck
He hates my guts so fuck my luck,
I'll kill the fucker so I will.
Fucking arseholes here he comes,
Garbage from the fucking slums.
He'd kiss my arse in Civvy Street
And call me 'sir', the little shite –
Look out China! On your feet,
He's coming over . . . 'Yes Sarge! Right!
Right away Sarge! Very well!
At the double . . . I'll do my best
Yes Sarge . . . Right Sarge – ' Fucky nell
I hope to fuck he was impressed.
You never know, the fucker might
Tear that 252 to bits
And I'll get pissed tomorrow night
Instead of doing fucking jankers –

But no! All NCOs are shits
And fuck-pigs, ponces, poufs and wankers.
He'll never let me off that charge –
'Right! I'm coming jildi Sarge!'

Varieties of Bastard

Not a bad old bastard, Captain Treve.
He only give me seven days CB
For being two days absent without leave.
That bastard what was previous OC
Would sling you in the bastard nick for less.
He give me fourteen bastard days last time
Because they said my bed-space was a mess!
What would he give you for a proper crime?
It's a bastard when your Company OC
Detests your bastard guts. When he got sent
To BHQ I shed no tears, not me.
Life's been all right since then. Old Treve's a gent
Compared with him. The CSM's not bad:
The bastard's strict but fair. And Sergeant Green's
A decent bastard underneath. I'm glad
It's his platoon I'm in and not McQueen's.
By Christ, McQueen's a proper bastard, mate.
You'd have to go to Hell to find one worse,
And there he'd be contender at his weight:
Corporal Watson's gentle as a nurse,
As nice a bastard as you'd wish to meet,
And all the lads is just about the best
Bunch of bastards you could find, a treat
To soldier with.   All right, get dressed.
Stop wasting bastard time. We'll get to town
Just as the pubs is opening, if you shift
Yourself a bit. Then first of all we'll down
A dozen pints of bitter pretty swift
And then we'll get some crumpet at the dance.

Can't dance? I know you can't. No more can't I.
But that don't mean we got no bastard chance
Of picking up some bints, and that's no lie.
And if the bastards brush us off we'll wait
Outside the bastard hall, and if they've got
Their boyfriends with them all the better, mate.
We'll get both effs – a fuck and fight, that's what!
Come on then, you old bastard, let's be quick.
I tell you, mate, of all the bastards in
The whole battalion you're the one I'd pick
To be my right-hand man through thick and thin.

F. F. I.

'Get fell in for F.F.I.!'
'What's F.F.I. mean Sarge?'
'You'd better call me Sergeant or
You'll find you're on a charge.'

'Sorry Sergeant'
                'All right son,
F.F.I. means free
From horrible infections like
Scabies and V.D.

'Now listen. If you've copped a dose
Of syphilis or clap
Don't claim you caught it from the seat
Last time you had a crap.

'The M.O. might be stupid like
Most officers and gents,
But don't believe that even them
Is total innocents.

'The quack, he knows about these things,
So just take it from him:
The only way to get poxed up
Is from an arse or quim.

'There's only two men in this mob –
And this you ought to know –
Who *can* catch pox from toilet seats:
The Chaplain and M.O.'

Rifle Inspection

My God, your rifle's manky!
You're on a fizzer lad!
I don't know what you think you're at!
You'll drive me bleedin' mad!

Both sights is fucking filthy!
There's spiders up the spout!
Last time you used it on the range
You never boiled it out.

You what? You lost your pull-through?
Right then, you must expect
Another charge as well as this –
Losing by neglect.

You're for the high-jump, sonny;
I almost pity you.
Meanwhile you'd better beg or steal
Pull-through and four-by-two.

What's the thing they learn you
At your mother's knee?
The best friend of a soldier's his
Lee Enfield 303!

Your best friend is your rifle:
So don't you let me see
You treating yours as if it was
Your bitter enemy.

Yes, treat it like your sweetheart,
Your baby or your wife.
Look after it! Maybe one day
The thing will save your life.

But now you're on a fizzer,
And when your pals is free
Tomorrow night to go to town
You'll find you're on CB.

And you'll be doing jankers
When they're out on the piss.
All right platoon: be warned by this!
Attention and dismiss!

Words of Command

Squad . . .	shun!
Right . . .	dress!
As . . .	you were!
Stand at . . .	ease!
Squad . . .	shun!
You . . .	yes!
You . . .	son!
You're a . . .	mess!
Get off . . .	your knees
Straighten . . .	up.
Stand at . . .	ease!
Squad . . .	shun!
Slope . . .	arms!
Squad . . .	will move
To the right in . . .	threes
Right . . .	turn!
By . . .	the left
Quick . . .	march!
Lef' . . .	righ'!
Lef' . . .	righ'!

That man there!
You look like a tart!
You might have broke
You old mum's heart
But mine, my lad,
You'll never break!

Lef' . . .	Righ'!
Lef' . . .	Righ'!
Eyes . . .	Righ'!
Eyes . . .	front!
Left . . .	wheel!
Mark . . .	time!
Forward . . .	march!
Squad . . .	halt!
Left . . .	turn!
Order . . .	arms!
Stand at . . .	ease!
Stand . . .	easy!

Oh my God,
Won't you never
Get to learn!
In all my days
I've never seen
Such a cheesy
Manky squad.

All right . . .	Squad!
Stand at . . .	ease!
Squad . . .	shun!
Order . . .	Christ!

I never said
Throw your rifle
On the deck!
Fucky Nell!
Pick it up
And watch your head
Don't fall off.
More sleep at night,
Less blanket-drill
And then you might
Do your stuff
And get it right.

As you were!
I will repeat
What I have told
You fifty times
At least before.
You must wait
Until you hear
The word of command.
You understand?
On no account
Anticipate.

All right . . .   once more.
Stand at . . .   ease!
Squad . . .   shun!

Thank God we've got
The Navy or
We'd never win
This fucking war.

Remembering El Alamein

Now listen, you young swaddies
Before they call Lights-Out,
I'll tell you a piece of history
You ought to know about.

Jerry and the Eyeties
Were knocking at the gate
Of Cairo with their pork swords fixed,
All set to celebrate.

They thought they'd walk right through us,
Our defences down the drain,
But they didn't reckon with the Jocks
That night at Alamein.

You've heard about old Monty's
Eighth Army, Desert Rats,
The Kiwis, Tynesiders and Guards
Led by aristocrats.

But the boys that really did it,
The ones that turned the tide,
Was the Highland Div., the Fifty-First,
And many of them died.

The first night of the battle
There was a fat white moon;
The stage was set and brightly lit
When the guns began to boom.

Our own twenty-five pounders
Flashed along the line;
They banged and roared and screamed until
They seemed to freeze your spine.

Your teeth began to chatter
Like Spanish castanets;
Your skull was bursting with the noise;
You froze in silver sweat.

And then we heard thin whistles
And orders to advance;
We moved through cordite mist and smoke
In a kind of nightmare trance.

We reached the enemy minefield;
The Scorpions had smashed through
And cleared a path that led us on
To the job we had to do.

And at the gap one piper
Played *Highland Laddie* for
Our comfort and encouragement,
Like a ghost from another war.

Of course that brave young piper
Did not stand there long;
Shrapnel or a Spandau-burst
Ended that brief song.

And then there was no music
Except the battle din:
The huge percussion of big guns
With small-arms rattling in.

And the worst sound in a battle
The noise that I still hear:
The voices of your comrades raised
In agony and fear.

I say that I still hear it;
I hear it in the night,
In dreams or when I'm just awake,
In darkness and in light.

That cry of dreadful knowledge,
The impossible come true;
The black thing that devours the rest
Has sunk its teeth in you.

I won't go on much longer;
It must be near lights-out;
But I want you all to understand
What I'm going on about.

It's this: there is no glory
In battle, only pain
And terror and the knowledge that
The dead have died in vain.

Twelve days the battle lasted
Before the enemy fled;
The air was spiced with that sick stench,
The sweet reek of the dead.

They never used a piper
To urge us on again;
Other tasks were found for them
After Alamein.

And don't think all was finished
When those twelve days were done:
For that was just the opening round
Of a contest not yet won.

We had to chase the bastards
For three months up the blue,
All the way to Tripoli,
And then still more to do.

Jerry dug in at Mareth;
But at last he had to run,
Though not before we'd planted more
Crosses in the sun.

It stabs my heart recalling
The good lads who were slain,
Who lie now in the rocks or sand
Of that forlorn terrain.

But of all the silent sleepers
Who rest on ridge or plain
I grieve most for the ones who died
At the start of Alamein.

Too young for such a finish –
It's hard to hold back tears
To think they drowned in endless dark
With the skirl of the pipes in their ears.

Sanitation Wallah

I joined up in the 'thirties, like
    Lots of other blokes
Who couldn't get a bleedin' job.
    I never told my folks
But signed my soul away to get
    A pint and twenty smokes.

The King's Shilling's what they give you then,
    Once you signed your name
And sold yourself like merchandise –
    I'd only myself to blame,
And if I'd a known what was to come
    I'd a joined up just the same.

It's not that nature meant me for
    A soldier's life, that I
Was made of the stuff of military men
    What say they'd sooner die
Then let the name of the regiment down,
    That's not the reason why.

I suppose I can't imagine life
    In civvy street at all;
I don't know how you ever get up
    Without revalley call;
Truth is, a soldier never grows up
    Though he might be six feet tall.

The army, it looks after you,
　　Just like a bleedin' nurse,
Though a bit more heavy-handed like
　　And more inclined to curse.
It feeds and clothes and tucks you up:
　　Things might be a damn sight worse.

Although I'm London born and bred
　　I joined a Scottish crowd.
My ancestors, you see, was Scotch –
　　My name is Jim Macleod –
And when I first put on the kilt
　　By Jesus, I was proud!

The other blokes all laughed at me
　　And called me Sassenach
And other things much less polite:
　　I don't blame them, looking back.
I wasn't one for making pals,
　　Just hadn't got the knack.

Stirling Castle was the place:
　　We learned to move in threes,
Did weapon-training, drills and guards
　　And got down on our knees
To scrub a hundred barrack floors
　　Before going overseas.

Egypt suited me all right;
　　I've always liked the heat;
And, when the Padre chose me for
　　His batman, life was sweet:
All I had to do was keep
　　His kit all clean and neat.

The cushiest job you'd ever get;
 Trust me to ruin it!
He used to leave his cash around;
 I only took a bit,
A few bob now and then, but he
 Split on me, the shit!

I lost the job of course, but worse
 I had a two-month spell
Of pack-drill at the double in
 That place next door to hell
They call Detention, where I slept
 On stone in a reeking cell.

I done my time and then went back
 To what life was before
The cushy batman's job, except
 I now was even more
Unpopular with everyone.
 Then came the bloody war!

I didn't think, when I joined up,
 I'd ever have to fight.
One taste of it was quite enough;
 I never dreamt that fright
Could chew you up and spit you out
 The way it did that night.

Our mob was ordered to attack;
 Sidi Barrani, the place.
The night was cold, a vicious wind
 Flung sand in every face
And choked and blinded us as we
 Advanced at walking pace.

Machine-gun bursts and eighty-eights
    Chattered, roared and flashed;
I heard the wounded wailing loud:
    Those bodies had been smashed
As mine at any moment might
    Be broken, gored and gashed.

Well, I survived that night somehow
    But on the following day
I took my old Lee Enfield, then
    I blew two toes away:
I'd swear it was an accident
    Whatever they might say.

It did the trick. I never saw
    No action after that.
When I came out of hospital
    They called me filthy rat
And things much worse but, at the base,
    I prospered and grew fat.

They made me sanitation wallah,
    And that's what I shall be
Until my time's expired for good,
    And it will do for me.
We all end up as we deserve:
    We *are* our destiny.

A sanitation wallah is
    The lowest of the low;
He cleans the men's ablutions and
    Each morning has to go
And empty all the chocolate-pots –
    Not soldier's work, I know.

But I think it is much better than
    Slogging up the blue
And digging in, scared shitless, when
    They've got a line on you,
Or lying in a shallow grave,
    Or I think I think I do.

Detention Wallah

'What did you do in the war Daddee?'
    'Lots of jankers, son:
Coal fatigues and scrubbing floors,
    Bashed spuds till I looked like one.

'Guards and pickets, rifle range,
    Chucking Mills grenades;
Kit-inspections, FFI's,
    Lectures and parades.

'Weapon-training – mortar, Bren –
    Forced marches at the double;
Bayonet-practice and PT,
    And never out of trouble.

'Always getting pegged for crimes
    Like dirty brasses or
An idle bootlace, petty things
    Is what they did me for.

'The officers and NCOs,
    They had it in for me;
When other lads was out on pass
    I was on CB.'

'But what about the war Daddee
    When the fighting started?'
'I took a powder, sonny-boy.
    I hastily departed.

'I wasn't going to get myself
        Blown to smithereens.
They'd never get me on that boat
        By any kind of means.

'I shoved my towel and shaving gear
        In my small pack and ran.
I got a lift to London in
        A big removal van.

'The red-caps, they soon picked me up;
        I got three months detention;
The glass-house, son, is hell on earth –
        There's things I just can't mention.

'Everything you do is done
        Always at the double;
That means you never walk, but run,
        Or else you're in real trouble.

'Each day I scrubbed the barrack-square
        Before PT began,
Down on all fours – if not a dog,
        Then something less than man.

'PT, son? What is that, you say?
        It's supposed to make you fit.
Pure Torture's what we knew it as,
        Whatever *they* called it.

'The whole idea, you see, was this:
        To make you suffer so
That even if Hell lay outside
        You'd volunteer to go.

'Not me though, son. I thought, "OK
        You treat me like a brute –
Those hours of packdrill, insults, blows
        And putting in the boot – "

'Lots of that there was, my lad.
        They'd beat you till you bled
And stick you into solitary
        With water and dry bread –

'"You treat me like an animal
        And that's just what I'll be,
Cunning, tough and obstinate:
        You'll never master me!"

'They never did, though I done more
        Glasshouse time than most;
So long I spent in solitary
        I came out like a ghost.

'But son, my spirit, underneath,
        Survived it all intact;
They thought they'd crushed me like a bug
        But I had won in fact.'

'But Daddee, what if everyone
        Had done the same as you?
We would have lost the war, Daddee,
        And lost our country, too!'

'If everyone had been like me
        No war could have occurred;
That's logic, son, can't be denied
        So take your old Dad's word.'

Old Sweat
or The Gift of
Tongues

Get some service in;
Your knees aren't brown yet, lad.
I might not be as old but I'm
Smarter than your dad.

So don't you try and come
The wide-o, clever dick.
Don't use them long posh words with me:
Your voice gets on my wick.

You haven't got no pips,
So talk the way we do.
That lah-di-dah will make the blokes
Piss all over you.

So drop them fancy airs,
You know they make me mad.
When you was in your Daddy's bag
I was in Baghdad.

Because I've got no rank
Don't mean I've got no sense.
When I complain you're like a kid
I don't mean no offence.

I just mean you don't know
The how and where and why
Of proper soldiering at all:
Your number isn't dry.

I've served in foreign parts –
You wouldn't know the names –
I speak the lingos and I know
The wogs's little games.

Experience is what
Learns you more than schools
And colleges that turns out squads
Of educated fools.

How many of them speak
Six languages, like me?
French, German, Arabic as well
As Itie and Parsee.

You what? That's only five?
I'm well aware of that.
The sixth one's what I'm talking now
You dozey little prat.

You might know Greek and Latin,
But let me tell you, pal,
Them's useless in Bombay or here
Beside the Sweet Canal.

Compree mon Kamerad?
Jig-jig, parley-voo,
Shufti zubrick, quois-kateer
San fairy ann, napoo.

Achtung, maleesh, sai-eeda,
Mafeesh faloose, buckshee;
Juldi, wahled, mangarea,
Promenade sheree.

Ears and eyes wide open
That's the way it's done;
Shut your trap, put in some time,
You'll be a man, my son.

Twelve-Hour Pass

I'm beezing up my toe-caps and I'm shining all the brass;
Buttons, cap-badge, gleam like gold; I'm on a twelve-hour pass.
Last night I pressed my strides between my bed and palliasse.
It's true I'm just a lance-jack but I've got a bit of class.
I've used white chalk on my one stripe and shaved and
    trimmed my tash;
I'm off to town. This time I swear I'll get myself a bash.
My hair is slick with brilliantine; I mean to cut a dash.
Tonight at the Astoria I bet I make a splash.
Bints like a man in uniform, or so folk always say;
I'm all set up, I look a treat, I've got a full week's pay.
If I pick up a bint tonight and she don't want to play
I swear I'll put one on her chin and shag her anyway.
That might sound hard, but so is life, and everybody knows
A bint says No when she means Yes, and that's the way it goes.
They get what they deserve and what they really want from you;
They've only got themselves to blame; we all know this is true.
There's nothing they like better than getting took by storm,
Pertickly if the man is one that wears a uniform.
Well, cheerio and wish me luck; tonight's the night, lads, so
With swagger-stick and blancoed prick I'm off to meet the foe,
'Cos we all know the enemy is not the Kraut or Jap;
It's that pretty little honey-pot with furry booby-trap.

Drinking Song

Tonight's the night so, by the right,
Right wheel! Then sink your liquor.
We're on the town; I've half-a-crown,
But Jim's got half a nicker.

We'll spend the lot no matter what
We feel like at revallee;
Them that think it's wrong to drink
Is sissy or dulallee.

Another bar, another jar,
No time for idle chatter;
We've had our fill of guards and drill
And now we're on the batter.

So drink up, son, we'll have some fun,
And when they've shut the boozers,
A bloke or dame, it's all the same,
Us buggers can't be choosers.

But, while they serve what we deserve
And much prefer to crumpet,
We'll kill our thirst with rapid bursts
As long as they will pump it.

So one last toast: the Holy Ghost,
Pure spirit, so they tell us;
The Padre he can get if free,
But I'm not really jealous.

Fill up your glass; this is our Mass –
See how the bottles glitter –
We are content, our sacrament
Potato-crisps and bitter.

THREE LOVE SONGS

1 *The Sentry's Song*

Fist clamps frozen on the rifle;
Frost and north-east malice stifle
All desire;
When the duty-stint is ended,
Flesh and soul will be attended
By kind fire.

Warmth and rest, and then soft dreaming;
Images of love's sweet scheming
Re-awake
Those intensities of yearning
Which set mind and body burning
For her sake.

Guardroom, uniform, and webbing
Fade and drift away; their ebbing
Leaves a bright
Shore where man and woman wearing
Mufti of silk skin are pairing
In delight.

2 *The Corporal's Song*

O, Dolly dear, you're more to me
Than my third stripe. I long to be
Close to you and once more see
Your eyes, their starry beauty;
Those other things I ache to do
I hardly dare confess to you:
I'll love you always – that is true –
Beyond the call of duty.

The lads in my platoon would grin
If they could see what happens in
My head but they could not begin
To understand love's power.
They think I am a man of steel
And could not guess at what I feel,
That X-Rays of my heart reveal
A single, fragile flower.

So roll on next weekend, my sweet;
I'll get a pass and we will meet
As always on Victoria Street,
And I shall hold you tightly.
O love, it seems too long to wait;
At times I feel I almost hate
This life that keeps us separate,
Prevents our loving nightly.

And yet, when all is said and done,
There's nothing like the roar of gun
And rifle's spite when war's begun
To make a soldier frisky.
The man who flirts with death and life
Is one who can excite his wife,
Like gleam and danger of a knife,
Make loving sweet, but risky.

3 *The Defaulter's Song*

Although I miss you, dearest heart
I would not have you with me here
To see me play this clownish part
Clad in penitential gear.
More than pain or loss I fear
Humiliation's sickly taste:
The sky seems one enormous sneer
As I crouch here, ashamed, abased.

I'm peeling spuds, enough to serve
A hundred hungry men. I feel
That this is worse than I deserve,
This scullion's role. I did not steal,
And tried my hardest to conceal
My lack of keenness to become
The sergeant-major's sworn ideal –
Unquestioning and blind and dumb.

Of course you never thought of me
As hero or as fighting-man.
There was a time I tried to be
Dead regimental but that plan
Was blown to bits when I began
To fall in love with you, my sweet.
Now nothing could be dearer than
A nest for us in civvy street.

I'll peel away like wedding-bells,
And do my jankers with a grin.
I think of you and my heart swells –
And something else – my senses spin
To dream of when we can begin
Our life together when we're wed
And you and I will snuggle in,
Like little spuds, our marriage bed.

Pipes and Drums

Slow, bandaged hammer-beat of drum is tolled,
Three booming spondees; pause, and then three more;
Then rattling side-drums chatter out their din,
Machine-gun rapid, as the pipes begin.

Pipe-major Mackie leads his men in march
And counter-march; kilts sway and swing; the wild
Barbaric voice of triumphs, griefs and fears
Floats dreams of banners, plumes and glittering spears.

Scotland the Brave, Hey, Johnny Cope, before
A change of tempo for the grave slow march:
The Flowers of the Forest are withered away, and then
The tunes of glory swagger out again.

The flagrant splendour still contrives to seize
The yielding heart; the mind almost believes
The tales this pageant tells, almost ignores
The excremental horror of all wars.

The pipers' boasts and lamentations fade;
Night and silence drape the barrack square.
A bugle sounds Lights Out; the last note dies,
Its sadness certain truth where all else lies.

Duff

Sloppy rice or semolina
Apple pie or stuff
Like spotted dick or roly-poly,
All were known as 'duff'.

One day I felt a bit off colour,
Couldn't eat at all.
I stayed behind when all the others
Answered cookhouse call.

I got my head down, shut my eyes,
But couldn't sleep a wink.
Then I heard the lads returning,
Voices, mess-tin clink.

I asked the first one back what dinner
Had been like. He said,
'Bloody awful. You did better
Staying in your bed.

'Of all the fucking awful dinners!
You'll never credit what
They give us for our duff: a fucking
Apple's what we got!'

Route March Rest

They marched in staggered columns through the lanes
Drowsy with dust and summer, rifles slung.
All other-ranks wore helmets and the sun
Drummed on bobbing metal pates and purred
Inside their skulls; the thumping tramp of boots
On gravel crunched. B Company had become
A long machine that clanked and throbbed. The reek
Of leather, sweat and rifle-oil was thick
And khaki on the body of the day.
All dainty fragrances were shouldered out
Though thrush and blackbird song could not be stilled
And teased some favoured regions of the air.

They reached a village and the order came
To halt and fall out for a rest. The men
Unslung their rifles, lit up cigarettes,
And sprawled or squatted on the village green.
Opposite the green, next to the church,
The school, whose open windows with wild flowers
In glass jars on the sills framed pools of dark,
Was silent, cool; but from the playground sprayed
The calls of children, bright as buttercups,
Until a handbell called them in from play
And then B Company was ordered back
To fall in on the road in their platoons
And start the march again.
                                        Beyond the church
They passed a marble plinth and saw the roll
Of names, too many surely for this small
Community, and as the files trudged on,
Faintly from the school, like breath of flowers
But half-remembered, children's voices rose:
'All things bright and beautiful,' they sang,
Frail sound, already fading, soon to die.

Church Parade

Faint breath of flowers but, overwhelming this,
A heavier scent of dust and holiness
As sunlight, strained through gold and purple glass,
Slants down to gild the altar and the cross.
An organ, sounding less than healthy, groans,
And slowly the Battalion, in platoons,
Files on heathen boots into the House
Of God. They settle, sheepish, in their pews.
Above the pulpit, on the wall, a board
Bears numbers like an oculist's testing-card.
Memories stir and tease; this heavy, sweet
Mysterious air and sound can propagate
Sensations from the treasurable past,
A nervous awe and momentary thirst
For goodness; boredom settling like the dust;
A sense of something frail and pure, now lost.

P.T.I.s

In the echoing gymnasium they shout,
Though 'shout' is too robust a word for those
Falsetto, yelped commands to stretch and bend;
There's something else androgynous about
The way they bounce and pirouette and pose:
Effects that few, if any, could intend.

Oddly insectile, too: their legs look thin
In hugging navy blue; their sweaters striped
In horizontal red and black, though each,
Whether dark or fair, possesses skin
That superfluity of health has wiped
Clean and lent the texture of a peach.

Despite big biceps and aggressive jaws,
That look of chorus-girl or model stays.
Their shiny stares are innocent of wit
Or curiosity; all human flaws
For them are physical, and their blank gaze
Is colder than the glass that mirrors it.

Casualty – Mental Ward

Something has gone wrong inside my head.
The sappers have left mines and wire behind;
I hold long conversations with the dead.

I do not always know what has been said;
The rhythms, not the words, stay in my mind;
Something has gone wrong inside my head.

Not just the sky but grass and trees are red,
The flares and tracers – or I'm colour-blind;
I hold long conversations with the dead.

Their presence comforts and sustains like bread;
When they don't come it's hard to be resigned;
Something has gone wrong inside my head.

They know about the snipers that I dread
And how the world is booby-trapped and mined;
I hold long conversations with the dead;

As all eyes close, they gather round my bed
And whisper consolation. When I find
Something has gone wrong inside my head
I hold long conversations with the dead.

War Graves at El Alamein

When they were little children they explored
Forests dense with dangers, were pursued
By beast, or giant wielding knife or sword
And terrified they found their feet were glued
Firmly to the ground; they could not scream
Or run, yet they were never stabbed or gored
But always woke to find it just a dream.

Years and nightmares later they became
Old enough to put on uniform,
And in parched throats they gagged upon the same
Taste of childhood terror in a storm
Of killing thunder they must battle through.
Now, unimportant pieces in the game,
They sleep and know that last bad dream was true.

Naming the Names

Carved on slabs of silence
    The litany of names
Outlives glass and palimpsest
    And time's lithophagous flames.

They cannot be buried in darkness
    With the white, staring dead
And their obsolete dreams and weapons;
    They cannot be unsaid.

Nor can we be deaf to the bitter
    Psalming of those nouns,
The names of the rivers and valleys,
    The broken, beautiful towns.

The Somme, like guns' far thunder,
    Ominous, yet with a sigh,
Passchendaele, Mons and Wipers,
    Graveyards where multitudes lie.

Arras, Bapaume, Vimy Ridge,
    The Marne, Loos and Cambrai,
Dark stains on the pitiful ribbons
    That will never fade away.

They are written in blood; and I wonder
    If those later slaughter-grounds
Dunkirk, Alamein, Arnhem,
    Will ever join these sounds.

Will my children's children tremble
   And sigh to hear them said,
And taste that bitter-sweet liquor
   Flavoured with pity and dread?

Or will the words be merely
   Names glanced at on a map?
Arromanches and Pegasus Bridge,
   Caen, the Falaise Gap.